Irish Family Treasures

Henry McDowell

IRISH FAMILIES

The story persists that most Irish records were lost in Irish wars and yet genealogical research continues apace, and many gaps in the archives have been filled by copies of documents – such as Wills – that have come to light in the offices of old firms of solicitors. Certainly many Protestant parish records were destroyed, and the shadow of the famine years hangs heavily over Catholic registers of the mid nineteenth century when the priest was sometimes moved to add a written comment on those terrible years.

It could be argued that successive invasion and strife left little time for the making and keeping of pedigrees when the Gaelic families together with the Anglo-Norman or 'Old English' settlers were uprooted and driven to the most remote parts of the country. It is known that Tirry or Terry, who was Athlone Herald at the Court of James II in exile, was much affected by the dearth of Irish records in the early eighteenth century, particularly when he was attempting to prove the ancestry of Irishmen who were about to marry into Continental noble families.

Today, Irish ancestry can mean many things besides Gaelic descent. Successive waves of invaders and settlers followed down the centuries, and most Irishmen have the blood of Elizabethan, Cromwellian or Scots planter somewhere in their pedigree. So much so that one can point to Irish presidents of English descent; Catholic bishops with Cromwellian names; and Anglican bishops with Gaelic ancestry who take pride in their ability to speak the Irish language.

The pattern of Irish emigration which was to continue for hundreds of years, began with the defeat of the Stuart cause in the eighteenth century; that of Charles II by Cromwell at Limerick in 1651, and forty years later of his brother James II by William of Orange at the Boyne. Soldiers of the old Gaelic and Anglo-Norman families left for the armies of the continent, and today the pedigrees of the chieftains are all found to contain references to members of the family with descendants long established in France, Spain and Portugal. The present chieftain of the O'Callaghans belongs to the Spanish branch who were finally recognised as the senior line as recently as 1944, although they first claimed the honour following the death – in a duel at Spancil Hill horse fair, Co. Clare, in 1791 – of Edmund O'Callaghan, who was described as 'extravagant and indolent, and in a constant state of pecuniary distress and embarrassment.' He left five daughters, one of whom married Lord Kenmare, owner of Killarney.

The extent of emigration from mid nineteenth-century Ireland to North America, is underlined by the recent publication of the third volume in the series *The Famine Immigrants*. This covers the short period from July 1848 to March 1849, when a total of 70,000 named Irish men, women and children disembarked at New York alone. Sometimes members of the same family lost touch with each other on arrival, and advertisements seeking contact appeared in the newspapers of Oneida County, New York. 'Moses Murphy arrived in U.S. May 1847, native of parish of Farens, Co. Wexford; worked as a book-keeper in New York City, intended to go to Ohio. Brother and sister now in Rome. Where is Moses?' *Rome Citizen* 1 Aug. 1849. Another advertisement from the pages of the *Utica Telegram* of 31 Aug. 1865, concerned 'Catharine White from Black-

water, Co. Kerry, came to U.S. about 15 years ago. Information on her wanted by her brother Timothy White at Lowville, Lewis Co., N.Y.' It is not unknown for the descendants of brothers and sisters to meet today, through their common interest in their Irish ancestry, and genealogical research is high on the list for many Americans and Australians visiting Ireland. Each summer sees increasing numbers working on their family history at the Public Record Offices in Dublin and Belfast, or moving around the countryside in search of headstones and cottage ruins. Success or failure in their quest for roots relies on the existence and state of preservation of parish registers in the area. Much depends on whether or not the entire family emigrated before or after Griffith's Primary Valuation, listing the occupier of even the smallest cabin, was recorded in the mid nineteenth century. Civil registration of birth, marriage and death began in 1864, so if the older generation remained in Ireland and died in the early years of registration, then the age recorded on a death certificate can give a useful lead to the approximate year of birth and the baptismal register.

Our great heritage of Georgian domestic and public architecture – with its unmistakable Irishness – was the outcome of a certain sense of stability in the land during the early eighteenth century. Fine houses were built and filled with Irish furniture; silver made in Dublin, Cork and Limerick; Waterford glass and portraits and landscapes commissioned from Latham, Slaughter and Ashford, and the family of painters known as Roberts. The pictures often filled specially designed ovals in the fine plasterwork, still to be found in both town and country interiors. Many such houses remained undisturbed into this century, only to be destroyed by fire during 'the Troubles' or more recently to have their contents scattered under the auctioneer's hammer. Of those that are left, a number of fine examples are open to the public and contain the kind of family treasures and curiosities illustrated in this booklet.

This brief selection of Irish families represents both Gaelic and settler. In almost all cases there is a variation of spelling, for example O'More, More and Moore, a name which can turn out to be either Gaelic *or* planter.

FITZ-GERALD

The first and most important of the Anglo-Norman Fitz-Geralds to come to Ireland was Maurice, who with ten knights, thirty men-at-arms and about one hundred archers and foot soldiers, landed in 1169 some months after his half-brother Robert FitzStephen, to fight on behalf of Dermot MacMorrough, King of Leinster. Maurice, Lord of Maynooth and Baron of Naas, died in 1176 and was the progenitor of all the Geraldines: the Earls of Desmond; the

White Knights; the Knights of Glin; the Knights of Kerry; and the greatest and most powerful of all, the Earls of Kildare and Dukes of Leinster. For many years the two great Fitz-Gerald Earls, Desmond and Kildare – together with the Butlers, Earls of Ormonde – virtually ruled Ireland. The English monarchs found it impossible to rule Ireland without their support and almost as impossible with it.

Thomas Fitz-Gerald, son of the 9th Earl of Kildare, led an unsuccessful rebellion against Henry VIII in 1535. As a result, Maynooth Castle lay in ruins, after a siege in which guns were used for the first time in Ireland and 'Silken Thomas' – so called because of the silk scarf he wore on the day he captured Dublin – was taken to England and executed at Tyburn. Undaunted, the Fitz-Geralds moved to Kilkea, the massive medieval fortress that dominates the wide and fertile Barrow valley in South Kildare. It was here in 1572 that the second son of the 11th Earl

The State bed has gone but the decorations of the Chinese Room at Carton have remained unchanged since 1759.

The galleried library is one of the most charming smaller rooms at Carton, Co. Kildare.

ordered a harp to be made and decorated with his monogram and Arms. This early Irish harp disappeared until the middle of the nineteenth century when a poor Dublin woman saw it at an auction and secured it for a modest sum. In turn, she sold it to Dr George Petrie, the historian, who gave it to Charles William 4th Duke of Leinster and so it returned to Kilkea. It can now be seen in the National Museum of Ireland.

In the easier and safer climate of the eighteenth century, the Kildare Fitz-Geralds built a great palladian palace at Carton, which became their principal seat. The size and grandeur of Carton reflected the continued political influence of the Fitz-Geralds and the elevation of the 20th Earl of Kildare, first to a Marquisate in 1761 and the Dukedom of Leinster in 1766. Emily Lennox, wife of the 1st Duke, decorated the state bedroom in the Chinese manner with hand-painted paper and Chinese Chippendale giltwood overmantle. After various vicissitudes Carton was sold in 1949 and much of the contents were auctioned off. Mrs

Blacker of Castlemartin bought the state bed, but unfortunately there was a high wind blowing as the Castlemartin farm lorry made its way home. The canopy and Chinese embroidered hangings were swept away and lost forever in an Irish bog. The Fitz-Geralds returned to Kilkea Castle until the present duke made his home in Oxfordshire.

Of all the noble Fitz-Geralds only one remains still living in his Irish castle. Desmond Fitz-Gerald, 29th Knight of Glin, or Glen, meaning the valley, descends from Sir John FitzJohn Fitz-Gerald who lived in the reign of Edward I. For 700 years, this family has held castles and lands on the south bank of the Shannon, across the estuary from Clare. The present castle was built in the late eighteenth century by John Bateman Fitz-Gerald, 24th Knight, and contains particularly fine and delicate Irish plaster work. The ceiling of the entrance hall, still in its original colours, incorporates symbols of the Irish Volunteers, and fine examples of native craftsmanship fill the beautiful rooms.

PLUNKET

Ireland's reputation as the land of saints and scholars remains true to this day. Blessed Oliver Plunket, Archbishop of Armagh and Primate of Ireland, martyred in 1681, was Canonised in 1975. St Oliver's ring and portrait are at the castle of Dunsany. This castle was originally built in about 1200 by the Justiciar of Ireland, Hugh de Lacy, whose main fortress was the largest Norman castle in Ireland – Trim – also in Co. Meath. The ruins of this magnificent stronghold still dominate the town on the banks of the Boyne. Sir Christopher Plunket married Joan, the only daughter of Sir Lucas de Cusack, Lord of Killeen in 1403. From this union there were two sons. John, the elder, inherited Killeen and is the ancestor of the Earls of Fingall, and Christopher was created Baron Dunsany. Edward Plunket, 12th Baron of Dunsany conformed to the Established Church in the eighteenth century, and so it was possible for him to prevent the forfeiture of his Catholic cousin's estate at Killeen. He swore ownership of it each year, until the passing of the Penal times. Following the recent death of Oliver Plunkett, 12th Earl of Fingall, his titles have devolved upon the 19th Baron of Dunsany thus reuniting the families of the two brothers, Christopher and John.

During the reign of Henry VIII, another branch of the Plunket family was elevated to the peerage as Barons of Louth. The battlemented façade of their ancient seat, Louth Hall, now stares grimly over the surrounding countryside. No Plunket has lived there for

In Irish houses, the staircase is sometimes made to fly past a Venetian window. At Dunsany, the eighteenth-century stairs rise grandly past several windows under a ceiling of delicate Gothic tracery.

more than fifty years, and the contents of the house were scattered long ago, at an auction sale.

The 11th Earl of Fingall, who died in 1929, is remembered for his classic definition of a gentleman: 'Any man is a gentleman who tells the truth and takes a bath once a day.'

Dunsany, a four-towered Pale castle enlarged in the eighteenth century.

In 1860, Lord O'Neill of Shane's Castle entertained his tenants as part of the celebrations to mark the coming of age of his eldest son, Edward. This event, recorded in watercolour, was on a big scale, as Lord O'Neill's County Antrim estates extended to 65,919 acres.

O'NEILL

Scholars agree that the greatest Irish dynasty is the Royal House of O'Neill, traceable to Eochu, King of Tara, living in AD 360. The name O'Neill, meaning grandson of Niall, was assumed by King Domnall in the tenth century and is the first surname to be adopted in Ireland. They reigned in Ulster until 1603, when Hugh, the Great O'Neill, 2nd Earl of Tyrone, was finally defeated by Lord Mountjoy and fled into exile with The O'Donell, 1st Earl of Tyrconnell. This was the celebrated 'Flight of the Earls'. His father, Conn the Lame, had been forced to submit after a long war to Henry VIII, who converted his kingdom into a mere earldom. The destruction of O'Neill power in Ulster over two generations heralded the Scots Plantation of their lands.

Today the recognised chieftain and head of the old Royal House of Ulster is a Portuguese nobleman. The Spanish representative of the O'Neills is the 11th Marques de la Granja and in Ulster the 4th Baron O'Neill of Shane's Castle, descendant of Mary the heiress of Henry O'Neill of Edenduffcarrick, who died in 1721, continues to live on his estate. Mary's grandfather, French John, built the family tomb at Shane's Castle. The inscription reads: 'This vault was built by Shane MacBrien MacPhelim MacShane MacBrien MacPhelim O'Neill, Esq., in the year 1722 for a Burial Place to himself and family of Clanneboy'.

Sir Niall O'Neill of Killeleagh, whose magnificent portrait is on the cover, raised O'Neill's Dragoons for King James II and 'signalised himself by his bravery'. He was at the Siege of Derry; faced some of Schomberg's army in Sligo in 1690 and displayed great valour at the Battle of the Boyne, where he was seriously wounded trying to hold the Ford of Rosnaree. Sir Niall was carried to Dublin and thence to Waterford where, owing to the carelessness of his surgeon, he died of his wounds at the age of thirty-two. J. M. Wright's portrait of Sir Niall, painted in 1680, shows this great Irish nobleman in his National dress of the period: 'With his "wild Irish" fringed cloak, curious but beautifully adorned Erse apron, long red hose, pointed brogues, Celtic dirk, basket-hilted broadsword, great oval shield of studded leather, gold-tipped black javelin, and elaborately-tooled leather conical cap with the flowing plumes of an Irish Chieftain.' His name appears in Gaelic characters on the dog's collar in the picture.

Shane's Castle, named after Shane McBrien O'Neill, and previously known as Edenduffcarrick, as it appeared in 1780.

LEESON

Hugh Leeson, the first member of the family to settle in Dublin, was a soldier turned brewer. Born in Northamptonshire, he married in 1673 Rebecca, daughter of Richard Tighe, a man from the same English shire who came to Ireland in 1640, and was Mayor of Dublin by 1651. The Tighes acquired much land and built Rosanna, a fine house in Co. Wicklow. On the strength of their brewing fortune, Hugh Leeson's only son Joseph, chose the same county of Wicklow as the setting for his much grander plans to build a mansion fit for a very rich man soon to be elevated to the peerage as Viscount Russborough and later Earl of Milltown. Alas, the male Leesons and their titles died out before the close of the nineteenth century.

Sir Alfred and Lady Beit saved a great Irish house by making their home at Russborough in 1952, and they alerted the art world about the four missing paintings commissioned from Claude Vernet in Rome, by Joseph Leeson in 1749/50. The four marine landscapes representing the seasons were intended to be an integral part of the decoration of Bindon's drawing room, completed after the death of the great Richard Castle, the German-born architect who settled in Ireland. These enchanting paintings disappeared at the time the estate was first sold in 1931 and were known to have passed through the hands of a Parisian art dealer before the Second World War. Thirty years went by before the pictures were rediscovered by Agnew and Sons of London. They were still in their giltwood frames and hanging – for almost all the years they were missing – in the New York apartment of an American stockbroker who was a well-known collector. Now, thanks to the Alfred Beit Foundation, everyone can visit Russborough and see Claude Vernet's masterpieces in the four plaster ovals envisaged by Bindon more than 200 years ago, in a house which is a living reminder of the high quality of eighteenth-century Irish craftsmanship.

For the genealogist, one question remains, where have all the Leesons gone and what about the dormant peerage of Milltown? In recent years a former railway employee, living in obscurity in India, put forward his claim to be Viscount Russborough and Earl of Milltown. He was unsuccessful.

A Harbour Scene *by Claude Vernet in its plasterwork surround at Russborough.*

The last of the Leeson connection, Lady Turton, sold Russborough to Captain and Mrs Denis Daly who lived there until 1951, when the property was bought by Sir Alfred and Lady Beit.

BAGWELL

The story of the Bagwells of Co. Tipperary follows the pattern of the settler family who put down roots and built a fine house which was completed in 1771. They owned most of Clonmel and in 1834, the traveller Henry Inglis recorded his impressions of the place. 'At once, on entering Clonmel, one perceives a hundred indications of an improving town. This is truly refreshing, after Kilkenny, Cashel, and many other wretched places I had passed through, and sojourned in.'

Richard Bagwell, the historian, was born at Marlfield in 1840. In his *Ireland under the Stuarts* he writes of the siege of the town in 1650. 'On April 27, Cromwell came before Clonmel and offered favourable terms, which were promptly rejected by the governor, Hugh Boy O'Neill, a nephew of Owen Roe, who had 1,500 Ulster men with him.' O'Neill, whom Cliffe describes as 'an old surly Spanish soldier' had expected to be attacked as far back as February, and Ormonde had written from Ennis at the beginning of March to say that he would 'draw all the forces of the kingdom into a body for the town's relief.' But he could do nothing, for the Commissioners of Trust were more anxious to thwart him than Cromwell, and would not allow a levy to be made in the county of Limerick. An attempt to send an expedition from the county of Cork was foiled by Broghill, and Clonmel was left to its fate. Preston had promised, but failed, to send ammunition from Waterford, and with Carrick in an enemy's hand it is not easy to see how he could have done so. O'Neill and the Mayor, John White, made a last appeal to Ormonde. The long threatened attack had come at last, and the preservation of the town was almost Ireland's last hope. 'It is,' they wrote, 'our humble suit that the army, if in any reasonable condition, may march night and day to our succour.' But no such army was available, and Cromwell planted his battery without hindrance. ... The assault was made about eight in the morning on 9 May, and the storming party entered without difficulty, but found that their work was still to do. O'Neill had manned the houses and erected two breastworks of 'dunghills, mortar, stones and timber', making a lane about eighty yards inwards from the breach with a masked battery at the

Dorcas Bagwell as painted by Angelica Kauffman, in 1771.

Marlfield, Clonmel, Co. Tipperary was completed in 1771 and rebuilt after the fire of 1923.

end. The 'British Officer', who got his facts 'not only from officers and soldiers of the besiegers', but also from the besieged, describes what followed. The stormers poured in and found themselves caught in a trap. Those in front cried 'Halt', and those behind 'Advance', 'till that pound or lane was full and could hold no more.' Two guns hailed chain-shot upon this dense mass, while a continual fire was kept up from the houses and the breastworks. Volleys of stones were thrown, and great pieces of timber hurled from the sides which O'Neill's ingenuity had provided, 'so that in less than an hour's time about a thousand men were killed in that pound, being atop one another.' Colonel Culham, who led the stormers, and several other officers were among the slain, and the survivors were driven out again through the breach. Contemporary accounts estimate Cromwell's total loss at Clonmel at somewhere from 1,500 to 2,500. This repulse, said Ireton afterwards, was 'the heaviest we ever endured either in England or here.' . . . Cromwell departed from Ireland on 26 May, leaving Ireton as his deputy.

When Marlfield was set alight by the anti-Treaty forces, on the night of 10 January 1923, Angelica Kauffman's portrait of Dorcas Bagwell was one of the few paintings to be saved. It had been commissioned by Colonel John Bagwell, M.P. for Co. Tipperary and builder of Marlfield, during the artist's only visit to Dublin in 1771–2. Senator John Bagwell accepted the offer of the newly founded Irish Free State to rebuild, and the picture returned to Marlfield until the property passed from the family in 1982. Today, the representative of the senior branch of the Bagwells of Marlfield lives and farms in New Zealand.

Dorcas Bagwell's marriage to Benjamin Bousefield was childless. Her great interest became building and then enlarging a 'Cottage Gothic', on land she inherited from her mother's family, the Harpers, overlooking a heavily-wooded backwater of Cork Harbour. With her nephew and heir, William Bagwell, who married Mary Spring-Rice, she planned the gardens and added what became known as the Wellington Tower. This new addition contained a large and impressive drawing room and a dining room with curved walls, for like many other established Irish families, the Bousefields anticipated a royal visit. The king never came to Eastgrove.

QUIN

The Quins of Munster are one of the few families of Celtic origin in the Irish peerage. Thady Quin, who was born in 1645, settled at Adare on the River Maigue, in Co. Limerick, where his son Valentine built a house in the early eighteenth century, which was to remain the family home for 150 years. Thady Quin's great-grandson was created a baronet in 1781, and raised to the peerage as Baron Adare of Adare in 1800. With the marriage of Lord Adare's son to the great heiress, Caroline Wyndham of Dunraven in Glamorganshire, the family assumed the surname of Wyndham in addition to Quin, and in 1822, Caroline's father-in-law who was already a Viscount, chose Dunraven and Mountearl as his title when he was granted an Earldom. The 2nd Earl was devoted to a sporting life until he became crippled with gout, so in 1832 he turned his mind to building a new house in the Tudor-Revival style, nearer to the river in his park at Adare. To begin with, Lord and Lady Dunraven acted as their own architects, and work was to continue for thirty-odd years. In 1845, James Pain, the professional architect, was called in, and later A. G. Pugin was commissioned to design some of the interior features. An inscription reads: 'This goodly house was erected by Windham Henry, Earl of Dunraven and Caroline his wife without borrowing, selling or leaving a debt, AD 1850.' Finally, the garden front was completed for the 3rd Earl between 1850 and 1862, by P. C. Hardwick. When a sale of the contents of Adare Manor took place in 1982, there was very considerable interest and demand for Pugin's work, and even his functional oak washstands fetched high prices. Paintings of race horses by D. Quigley (fl. 1750–73) were included in the sale, and a fine example showing the jockey wearing the racing colours of Windham Quin of Adare (1717–89) against a background of the cathedral of Kildare and the ancient round tower beside it, was purchased by the National Gallery. The Curragh of Kildare was then as now used for the training and racing of horses. Valentine Quin of Adare was an executor of the Will, dated 26 August 1765, of Sir Edward O'Brien of Dromoland who was a racing man. To his third son, also Edward O'Brien, he left all the rest of his horses, mares, colts and fillies. As he may want stable room and grass for them 'when my head is under a stone,' he leaves him his interest in the stables and lands of Jockey Hall near the Curragh; also 'my gold snuffbox with a galloping horse chased on the lid. . . .'

Paintings of favourite horses and dogs abound in Irish country houses, and the picture of the Dunraven Dog with Quin Abbey and Adare demesne in the background must have hung in the eighteenth-century house built by Valentine Quin. In his memoirs, the 5th Earl who died in his ninety-sixth year in 1958, tells us that his grandparents kept pulling down the old house, bit by bit, until a few rooms of the new house were ready for occupation, and when they moved across the park the portrait of the Dunraven Dog went with them. Now the painting has followed the family to their new home not far from the picturesque village of Adare.

James Quin was a bearer of the name who won international recognition. He was a grandson of Mark Quin, Mayor of Dublin in 1676. He was born out of wedlock and destined to be a great Shakespearean actor. James Quin (1693–1766) made his name on the London stage, where he rivalled Garrick, and it was not until Quin's retirement that the actors became

The Black Dog of Adare, *painted by an unknown artist, with the Franciscan Friary in the background.*

friends when they met under the same roof, staying with the Duke of Devonshire at Chatsworth. James Quin's first appearance was at the Smock Alley Theatre where the church of SS Michael and John now stands, and he returned to Dublin in the autumn of 1741 to play Cato at the Aungier Street Theatre. His portrait by Hogarth hangs at the Tate, and another by Gainsborough is in Buckingham Palace. Horace Walpole admired his wit and used many of his stories. On his death, a lying biography was published and some of the scandalous details have been copied into collections of memoirs. James Quin was amused by society. Dining with the Duchess of Marlborough and finding that she ate no fat of venison, he exclaimed, 'I like to dine with such fools.'

Finally we come to St John Thomas Quin, a romantic figure if ever there was one. In 1814 he dedicated his poems, one of which was composed 'while the author lay ill of a fever' to Miss Bonynge. These included 'Romantic Tales' and other pieces, 'The Mountain of the Lovers', and 'Eveline'; or the 'Nun of Knockmay'. The final verse in St John Thomas Quin's manuscript concerns his Irish harp.

Adare Manor – the Great Gallery measures over 40 metres and has now lost its contents under the auctioneer's hammer.

> Where is the much loved harp that
>   oft before
> Was used the poet's sorrowing
>   breast to cheer?
> Alas, that harp can soothe his cares
>   no more
> For every string is rusted with a
>   tear!

A watercolour of Castle Donovan commissioned by Dr John O'Donovan, the well-known scholar, in 1843 as a present for Morgan William, The O'Donovan.

O'DONOVAN

Few chieftans are as fortunate as The O'Donovan who has a verified pedigree from Gaelic times, beginning with Cahal, Chief of Hy Fidhgeinte, killed by Callaghan Cashel, King of Munster AD 964. Donal-of-the-Hides – so called because as a child he was wrapped in cow hides to conceal him from his father's enemies – was succeeded in 1584, by Donal O'Donovan, The O'Donovan, 9th in descent, the builder of Castle Donovan in the Hills, near the village of Drimoleague in the Barony of West Carbery, Co. Cork. Although the castle and lands were taken by Cromwell, the Privy Council directed that O'Donovan was to have his estates restored in 1661. Unfortunately, Charles II confirmed Castle Donovan and 1,465 acres to a Cromwellian officer named Nathaniel Evanson, and the family regained only a part of their property. In 1689, O'Donovan was still agitating for the return of his lands, yet despite his grievance he raised a regiment of infantry to fight for King James, and his defence of Charlesfort at Kinsale, won him a considerable reputation as a soldier. After the capitulation he surrendered the keys into the hands of the Earl (later Duke) of Marlborough, and on 12 October 1691, he was ordered to march with his regiment to Cork for embarkation to France. The question remains – Did Colonel Daniel O'Donovan, actually go to France? On 4 January 1692, a pass was issued to permit him to travel to Timoleague and thence to Cork to deliver himself a prisoner, but on the available evidence it is not certain if he was then in Ireland. In 1693 and again in December 1694, O'Donovan was making efforts to have his attainder lifted. He was to live on into the eighteenth century when his son, Richard, married Elinor Fitz-Gerald, daughter of the 13th Knight of Kerry.

Seventeenth-century silver tankard uncovered in the bog at Castle Donovan by an old man cutting turf in the last century.

The Arms of O'Don

árvisfidh

egiollaiosachta,
, beannacht.
Winthrop
an Chornail
Lios Árd, An
riam Contae
nnabhán as
e, Scríbhéar,
alais mar
is go bhfuil
-iompar le
un sé an
adh cheana
leis go
dleathach
fhoillsithe
eile, agus a
ar na Sine
aí is cuibhe
is sin ar na
chur ar
naidh na hOifigigh
mar is gá iad do
alas do chur orthu.
eithniú agus na dála
il liom-sa, Príomh
ráibhinn seo agus ag
húdarás Rialtais
o dhaingniú don
abhán sin, eadhon:
dearg-éaduithe le
ch as clé na scéithe
r-chlaidhimh go
raon dualdaithe:
órdha ag tuirling:
each agus ar chlé
nte Deo in Hostes
eith ag éinne ach
le linn a bheatha.
o theachtadh don
bhán sin agus dá
, dá úsáid, dá
sin ar scéith nó ar
gus ag úsáid a
lithe Armais agus
gan coisceadh gan
hoinibh ar bith.
nn agus mo theideal
ige dhe an dara lá

To All

shall come, I, Ed
Principal Heral
Whereas ap
Brigadier Mor
son of Colonel W
Liss Ard, Skibber
descended from
Co. Cork, Esquire,
Office as Chief of
Armorial Ensig
his family wh
heretofore reco
them, and furth
that such Arm
prejudice to an
may be duly e
and praying t
full confirma
aforesaid with
proper and th
confirmed ma
Office to the end the
there and all others w
and have knowledge
Now, I, the sai
having taken the sai
and having enquired i
am pleased to compl
by these presents, actin
of the Government of I
said **Morgan John W**
Ensigns following, tha
the sinister side of the
vested gules cuffed of th
with a serpent proper,
a falcon alighting or,
and sinister a griffin pr
Hostes, provided always
be used by the person w
To have and to hold the s
Winthrop O Donovan a
same to bear, use, shew,
banner or otherwise, obs
proper differences accor
and without the let, hind
controlment or challen
persons whatsoever.
In Witness whe
my Name and Title and
Office this Second day o

Towards the end of the nineteenth century, an old man cutting turf in the shadow of the ruin of Castle Donovan, came upon a silver tankard buried in the bog. It was made in 1696, by Robert Goble, silversmith of Cork, and bore the Arms of Daniel O'Donovan, The O'Donovan, 11th in descent and a Colonel in the service of James II.

O'BRIEN

Brian Boru (Boroimhe), King of all Ireland, was an old man when he met his death in his final and decisive battle at Clontarf in 1014, against the Danes, who were to retain their hold over England for thirty years after their expulsion from Ireland. The Annals of Innisfallen record that the Danes and their ally the King of Leinster lost 13,800 men; Brian Boru's dead numbered 4,000.

The O'Briens remained Kings of Thomond until 1543 when Morogh O'Brien submitted 'his Captainship, title, superiority and country' to Henry VIII at Greenwich Palace and was created Earl of Thomond and Baron of Inchiquin. His princely status was acknowledged by the right to bear on his shield the Royal Arms and to wear the Royal livery. Colonel Conor O'Brien of Lemeneagh, descendant of Conor O'Brien third son of Morogh, was killed by Cromwellian troops under the command of General Ireton in 1651, not far from his castle. His wife saved the family fortunes and estate from confiscation by a remarkable ruse. She was Mary daughter of Torlough Roe McMahon, known as Maura Rua (Mary of the Red Hair). In order that the family should not be dispossessed, she offered herself in marriage to any Cromwellian officer nominated by Ireton. Cornet John Cooper put himself forward and became her second husband. Maura Rua's only son Sir Donagh O'Brien, 1st Baronet, moved from Lemeneagh to the castle of Dromoland, taking with him the famous Armada Table. This massive piece of Spanish mahogany inlaid with ivory, came from the captain's cabin of one of the many galleons wrecked off the Irish coast, following Philip II of Spain's ill-fated attempt to invade England in 1588. The table may be seen at Bunratty, another O'Brien fortress, where medieval banquets are a considerable attraction. Dromoland Castle was rebuilt in the Gothic style in the nineteenth century, and is now a first-class hotel.

The Armada Table, now on loan to Bunratty Castle from Lord Inchiquin who lives at Thomond House in Co. Clare.

The Kilwarlins, *a sketch by George Moutard Woodward – 'Billy! why but you hit thon "Tingilur" and bate him out o' the pot – you'd let him ate the bottom out of it, before you'd hit him a clout – ! you're no huntsman – ! –'*

O'REILLY

'A good deal of unreliable material is to be found in print on the subject of the O'Reillys' warns Dr Edward Mac-Lysaght, and another great Irish genealogist, Father Patrick Woulfe points out that the family maintained their independence as a clan down to the time of James I, and continued in possession of considerable property until the Cromwelliam confiscations. Dr MacLysaght adds that they were not exactly landless in the nineteenth century when they still owned 30,000 acres. In 1923, a maid at an O'Reilly castle about to take her afternoon off, remarked: 'I'll not leave my bicycle – sure I wouldn't want to have it burned.' The family thought she was madder than usual – until the raiders arrived with cans of petrol at dusk.

George Moutard Woodward, carica-turist, and son of a Derbyshire squire, was a friend of John Reilly of Scarvagh, Co. Down, who represented a cadet branch of the O'Reillys of Knock Abbey,

descendants of the Princes of East Brefny. His sketch of 'The Kilwarlins' or Mr Reilly's Hounds was probably drawn towards the end of the eigh-teenth century, on a visit to Scarvagh. Woodward died penniless, of dropsy, in the Brown Bear public house, Bow Street, whose landlord had been chari-table enough to give him shelter.

The traveller, Arthur Young, has left us a description of life in the house-hold of a sporting and impoverished Irish landlord of the type that Woodward depicted in his drawings.

His hospitality was unbounded, and it never for a moment came into his head to make any provision for feeding the people he brought into his house. While credit was to be had, his butler or housekeeper did this for him; his own attention was given solely to the cellar that wine might not be wanted. If claret was secured, with a dead ox or sheep hanging in the slaughter house ready for steaks or cutlets, he thought all was well. He was never easy without com-pany in the house, and with a large

party in it would invite another of twice the number. One day the cook came into the breakfast parlour before all the company: 'Sir, there's no coals.' 'Then burn turf.' 'Sir, there's no turf.' 'Then, cut down a tree.' This was a forlorn hope, for in all probability he must have gone three miles to find one, all round the house being long ago safely swept away. They dispatched a number of cars to borrow turf. Candles were equally deficient, for unfortunately he was fond of dogs, all half-starved, so that a gentleman walking to what was called his bedchamber, after making two or three turnings, met a hungry greyhound who, jumping up, took the candle out of the candlestick and devoured it in a trice, and left him in the dark. To advance or return was equally a matter of chance; therefore groping his way he soon found himself in the midst of a parcel of giggling maid-servants. By what means he at last found his way to his shakedown is unknown.

After the Battle of the Boyne, Hugh O'Reilly ancestor of the O'Reillys of Westmeath, followed James II into exile at St Germain. The king appointed him Lord Chancellor of Ireland, an empty honour as his monarch had lost his kingdom and was totally dependent on Louis XIV. Hugh O'Reilly took up his pen in place of his sword, and wrote *Ireland's Case briefly stated, or a summary account of the most remarkable Transactions of that Kingdom since the Reformation*. The king, however, was far from pleased by this effort, and Hugh was deprived of both his titular office and the small stipend that went with it. The following year, 1694, he died of a broken heart. Back in Ireland, Hugh O'Reilly's descendants were to flourish and see better times on their Westmeath estates at Ballinlough Castle. His great-great-grandson, also Hugh, was created a baronet in 1795, and Sir Hugh's brother, Field Marshal Andrew O'Reilly in the service of Austria, was appointed Governor of Vienna in 1809. Sir Hugh O'Reilly, 1st Baronet, changed his name to Nugent on the death of his uncle, and the family continue as baronets of Ballinlough Castle to this day.

O CONOR

The library at Clonalis, near Castlerea in Co. Roscommon, is rich in early manuscript material relating to the royal family of O Conor, once Kings of Connaught, and from which dynasty came the last two High Kings of Ireland. A twelfth-century address to one of them begins: 'King of Connacht, Meath, Breifne, and Munster, and of all Ireland, flood of the glory and splendour of Ireland, the Augustus of Western Europe, a man full of charity and mercy, hospitality and chivalry.'

Roderic O Conor was King of Connaught and the High King when Strongbow invaded, but was forced by the Treaty of Windsor in 1175 to recognise the English king as Monarch and Lord Paramount of All Ireland, which he did in return for recognition as vassal King of Connacht. Two hundred years later, two cousins, both called Turlough O Conor, claimed the O Conor titles. In order to distinguish them, one was called O Conor Don and the other O Conor Roe. On the death of Roderic O Conor King of Connaught in 1384, the kingdom divided between the two Turloughs, each of whom claimed total sovereignty. The O Conor Dons, as the descendants of vasal kings continue as hereditary Standard Bearers of Ireland at the Coronations of the Kings of England in Westminster Abbey. The green standard, bearing the golden harp, which hangs in the entrance hall of Clonalis was last carried in 1911 at the Coronation of George V.

A fascinating and valuable description of the inauguration of Cathal Craobhdheargh O Conor of the Red Hand, as King of Connaught at Carnfree near Tulsk in 1201, written by an eye witness, shows the elaborate Court Ceremonial and the orders of Gaelic nobility. The writer records the bishops and chieftains required to attend and lists the hereditary appointments: 'It is the privilege of O Mulconry to place the rod in the hands of O Conor, the day on which he assumes the sovereignty of Connaught . . . the king's clothing and arms were given to O Mulconry, and his steed to O Flynn . . . an ounce of gold was decreed to O Connaghten as a perennial tribute, on condition of his repairing the carn when it required repairs. The following are the subsidies paid to the different chieftains of Sil Murray. Twelve score of milch cows, twelve score sheep and twelve score cows to O Flannagan, and the same number to Mageraghty and O Mulrenin. The office of High Steward was ceded to O Flanagan, O Hanly is the keeper of his hostages, and he had the command of

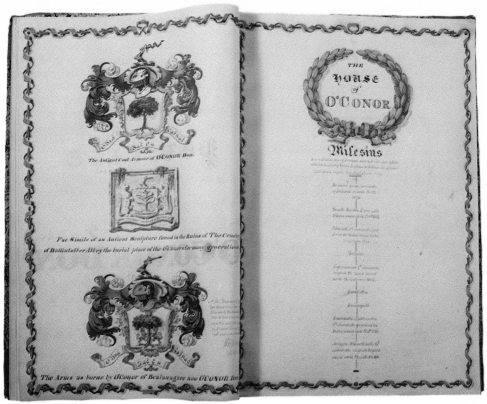

The Arms and Pedigree of the House of O'Conor, starting with Milesius.

A portrait of the learned antiquary and Chaplain to Lady Mary Elizabeth Nugent, wife of the first Marquis of Buckingham, the Very Rev. Charles O'Conor, D.D. (1764–1828), presides over the library at Clonalis.

nis fleet from Slieve-in-Iarain to Luimneach (Limerick) . . . MacBranan is his henchman, and chief of his kerne, and the caretaker of his hounds. MacDockwra is his procurator-General who is bound to furnish light and bedding . . . the chief command of O Conor's fleet belongs to O Flaherty and O Malley. O Kelly is the chief treasurer of his precious stones, and all other species of treasure. MacDermot of Moylurg is his marshal; O Teige the chief of his household, O Beirne his chief butler, O Finaghty his chief doorkeeper, O Mulconry the recorder of all his tributes, MacTully his physician, and MacEgan his brehon (judge).'

In a recent comment on the above, The MacDermot writes: 'It is extraordinary that despite conquest and emigration and the passing of eight hundred years, most of the families mentioned are still to be found on the same lands in Connaught.'

SOMERVILLE

Two grand-daughters of Chief Justice Charles Kendal Bushe, that great opponent of the Union, formed a literary partnership which was to make the names of Somerville and Ross and their ever popular stories of *The Experiences of an Irish R.M.* known to lovers of Ireland the world over. Both Edith Enone Somerville and Violet Martin of Ross, had a faultless ear for the dialogue of the country people, and in addition Edith was an artist and the illustrator of many of their books. Her family came to Ireland in 1690, when the Rev. William Somerville landed from an open boat in September of that year, at Donaghadee, Co. Down. He was fleeing from his parish in the stewardship of Galloway, escaping in fear of his life during the covenanting troubles in Scotland. His son, also a parson, established the Somervilles in West Cork where they have retained their link to the present day. Three sons of the third generation in Ireland, migrated to America where they founded the town of Somerville, New Jersey.

At Drishane, the house where Edith Somerville spent most of her life, there is a fairy shoe that was found in 1835 in a glen of the Caha range of mountains which divide the Kenmare River from Bantry Bay. It was discovered just after daybreak, by a man travelling across country on foot to fetch the doctor for his wife, who was ill. He picked it up in a wild and desolate place but was afraid to keep it, believing it to belong to the Little People. Edith took the shoe to America where she had it analysed, and it was declared to be made of mouse

The Fairy Shoe from Co. Cork is in the same league as the ffolliott Fairy Coat found in Co. Meath. When shown the latter, a tailor remarked, 'That coat, sir, was not made by mortal hand.'

Edith Œnone Somerville, Master of Foxhounds. One day, when she was hunting hounds, she spent nine hours in the saddle.

skin. It is considered to be a lucky talisman for Drishane.

Once, it was put in the bank for safe keeping and the cattle on the farm immediately fell into decline and did not recover until it was restored to its usual place in the house. In 1903, when Edith Somerville took office as Master of the West Carbury Hunt, she was the second woman in the history of fox-hunting in the British Isles to have this honour. She continued as Master until 1919, and her portrait in hunting clothes by John Crealock did not entirely please her. With her own paint brushes she altered the mouth, to a

firmer and stronger line.

Of all the books published under the names of E. E. Somerville and Martin Ross, the critics considered *The Real Charlotte* to be the best, and likened their style to that of Balzac. However, the most enduring and best loved remains *The Experiences of an Irish R.M.* which has been serialised for television most successfully.

KAVANAGH

The most famous of this family was Dermot MacMorrough, King of Leinster, who abducted Dovorgilla, wife of Tiernan O'Rourke, Lord of Brefny in 1152. Noted for both his cruelty and his piety, it was Dermot who sought the assistance of the English to recover his kingdom from O'Rourke. This appeal for help provided the perfect excuse for the Anglo-Normans. Henry II had contemplated invading Ireland some years previously, and had actually obtained from the only English Pope, Hadrian VI, a Papal Bull authorising such an expedition. Richard de Clare, Earl of Pembroke – known as Strongbow – landed in Ireland, defeated the Gaels, and married MacMorrough's daughter Eva. Dermot MacMorrough died in 1170. At the end of the following year, Henry II arrived to accept the feudal vassalage of both Strongbow and the Irish kings and chieftains.

Dermot was succeeded by his bastard son Donall, who submitted to the English crown in 1175, and received the celebrated Kavanagh Charter Horn in token of forgiveness. He was then permitted to hold his lands in fief from the king. Some experts consider the ivory and brass drinking horn to date from the thirteenth century, and it is possible that it was redecorated at the later date when the metal shrine holding another Kavanagh treasure – the Book of Mulling – was embellished for Art MacMorrough in 1403. The Horn may now be seen at the National

Borris House, Co. Carlow, home of Andrew MacMorrough Kavanagh, farmer, and grandson of Major Arthur MacMorrough Kavanagh, The MacMorrough.

Museum of Ireland, and the book is now in Trinity College Library.

The term 'Kavanagh's Country' was applied to the districts occupied by the family in the Middle Ages – much of counties Carlow, Wexford and Wicklow. Safety for English settlers was assured as long as an annual payment was made by the Dublin administration to the Kavanaghs. A denial of this frequently brought trouble and Richard II was twice forced to negotiate settlements with Art MacMorrough.

The ancestral home of the Kavanaghs is at Borris, in Co. Carlow. The moving love-song *Eileen a Roon* tells of the elopement of Eileen Kavanagh with her lover from Connaught, Cormac O'Daly. This occurred in the fourteenth century, her father having arranged a politically useful marriage with an Anglo-Norman. In the sixteenth century, Cahir MacArt Boy Kavanagh, Baron of Ballyanne, The Mac-Morrough, married Cecilia, a daughter of the 9th Earl of Kildare. Four hundred years later Gerald, Marquess of Kildare, now 8th Duke of Leinster, married Joane, daughter of Major Arthur Mac-Morrough Kavanagh, The MacMorrough, of Borris. In any study of Irish genealogy, relationships may be found between old families living for centuries in the same province.

The American poet, Richard Hovey, marked the hospitality at Borris with some verses dedicated to his host, Arthur MacMorrough Kavanagh (1831–89), who, although born with only rudimentary arms and legs, was a Member of Parliament and managed to lead an active life which included both sport and travel.

A stone jug and a pewter mug,
And a table set for three!
A jug and a mug in every place,
And a biscuit or two with Brie!
Three stone jugs of Cruiskeen Lawn,
And a cheese like crusted foam!
The Kavanagh receives to-night!
MacMorrough is at home!

O'MORE

In writing of the O'Mores, the former Chief Herald of Ireland, Dr Edward MacLysaght, draws our attention to the interesting fact that out of thirteen pedigrees of Moore in *Burke's Landed Gentry of Ireland* twelve claim to have come to this country from England or Scotland and only one to be an offshoot of the O'Mores of Leix. The portrait of Rory O'More of Leix – who is credited with starting nineteen rebellions in the seventeenth century – dominates the dining room of Roderic More O'Ferrall at Kildangan, Co. Kildare, who descends from the Ballyna O'Mores through Letitia More who married Richard Ferrall in 1751. The O'Mores of Leix were constantly in rebellion and fiercely opposed all attempts at settlement on their hereditary lands. In the mid fourteenth century the Norman castle built on the Rock of Dunamase and held by Roger de Mortimer, was destroyed by Lisagh O'More, who, in one night set on fire eight of the Norman's castles and banished the English from Leix. The O'Mores were such a scourge to the king's rule, that an

example was made of them when they could be captured. In 1578 the head of Rory Oge O'More was set on the walls of Dublin Castle. Three years earlier Rory had been forced to submit to Queen Elizabeth's Deputy, Sir Henry Sydney at Kilkenny Cathedral 'repenting his former faults and promising hereafter to live in better sort (for worse than he hath been he cannot be).'

The Colonel Rory in the portrait followed in the footsteps of his forebears. In 1641 after a skirmish at Julianstown where his men defeated the Government forces, a price of £400 was put on his head. Even though never captured, he was eventually forced to the Island fastness of Bofin in 1652 by Cromwell's troops. He may have died there, but there were reports that he had been seen, disguised as a fisherman, in Ulster where he was seeking passage to Scotland. The impressive portrait is by an unknown artist and is an example of an Irish heirloom which has descended 'through a series of changes'. It had previously hung at Balyna, where there is a legend that Rory plunged his staff into the ground and it took root, growing into a conifer. It was said that when the tree died the O'Mores and their descendants would cease to own Balyna. The tree fell in a storm in the 1950s, and not long afterwards the estate passed into other hands, after more than 300 years.

'Do you ask why the Beacon and Banner of War
On Ulster's Green Mountains are seen from afar?
Tis the signal our rights to regain and secure
Thro' God, Our Lady and Rory O'More.'
(old

THE IRISH HERITAGE SERIES

ISBN 900346–67–1
© 1985
Published by Eason & Son Ltd, Dublin
Printed in Great Britain by Jarrold & Sons Ltd, Norwich. 185

Front cover: *Sir Niall O'Neill of Killeleagh, painted by J. M. Wright in 1680.*

Flap – Top left: *Dinner plate bearing the monkey crest of Fitz-Gerald, Duke of Leinster, Marquis and Earl of Kildare, Chief of the Geraldines. Motto – Crom a boo.*

Flap – top right: *Decorative plate with Arms of Taylor impaling O'Brien.*

Flap – centre: *Faugh-A-Ballagh, winner of the St Leger in 1844, was owned by the Irwin family who commissioned a dinner service to celebrate the event, from Thomas and Higginbotham of Wellington Quay, Dublin.*

Flap – bottom: *Silver basket, presented in 1755 to Mrs Browne, daughter of Mountiford Westropp of Attyflyn, by William Miller 'in acknowledgement of her careful, tender and affectionate behaviour to an orphan child'.*

Inside flap: *The antlers of the extinct Irish Elk or giant deer, complete the decoration of the Tudor-Revival hall at Adare Manor.*

Back cover: *A montage of Fitz-Gerald family memorabilia arranged by the 29th Knight in the hall at Glin.*